SONGS FROM THE SOUTHERN OREGON COAST

Curated by Gary Carter

Published by Unsolicited Press

www.unsolicitedpress.com

Unsolicited Press Books are distributed to the trade by Ingram.

Editor: S.R. Stewart

ISBN: 978-1-947021-31-0

Cover design: UP Team

Font: Myriad Pro Condensed and Trajan Pro

FOREWORD

SONGS FROM THE SOUTHERN OREGON COAST was conceived to invite people from all over the world to visit the southern Oregon coast by letting them know how beautiful and historical this part of our world is.

Poets and short story writers were sought to express their views on why they choose to live along the southern Oregon coast. Their reasons are varied and many and all contributors, although expressed in different ways, have one thing in common: they agree that the Coos and Curry county coastlines are among the most beautiful, and interesting, places in the world. Come and find out for yourself!

DEDICATION

To Professor Barbara Drake, who resides in Yamhill County, Oregon, but also has a small home along the Sixes River Valley in Curry County, for suggesting I collect poems and stories from south coast authors about their experiences and what they love about living along the southern Oregon Coast and put them in a book for all to enjoy.

When she was a young girl Professor Drake and her family settled in Coos Bay, Oregon where she attended school at Marshfield High school. After graduating she earned her B.A. and M.F.A. degrees from the University of Oregon. She eventually moved to Michigan and taught at Michigan State University before returning to Oregon 16 years later. She taught at Linfield College before retiring in 2007.

Thank you Barbara!

To Megan Maloney, member of the Bandon Library Friends and Foundation, for encouraging the young people (grades 5-12) from Bandon, Langlois and Port Orford to submit poems or short stories to this publication.

Their contributions are compiled in a special section of "Songs" and cover a wide spectrum of their views on living along the Southern Oregon Coast.

Thank you Megan!

Also, thanks to all my friends and family who have encouraged and supported my writing over the years. Without them this book would never have been conceived, written or published.

Thanks most of all to our contributors. To hear all these different voices describing our corner of the world has been an incredible journey: enlightening, funny, sad, awesome, and amazing are just some of the words that come to mind. I hope everyone who reads this book has as much fun and joy as I have had in putting it together.

--Gary Carter

CONTENTS

SONGS FROM THE

SOUTHERN OREGON COAST

BLANCO: AN INVITATION

Professor Barbara Drake – Sixes River Valley

Come walk with me from Cape Blanco to the mouth of the Sixes,

a river of black sand and gold that long-ago miners followed for fortunes,

never richly granted but doled out in miniscule flakes of shining metal.

Have you heard the story about the man who lived upriver with two wives

mining the source of gold in the Sixes? He was suspicious

of anyone hiking that far who might abscond with his gold, or his wives.

The wives wore faded dresses made from old flour sacks,

and their plump bodies were covered with brown hair.

Apocryphal? Maybe not, this south coast never being quite settled.

Too poor and far from cities, too little populated,

steeped in Quiverran mythologies and Jeffersonian attitudes.

It is generally recommended, in these parts, that one stay clear

of a man with two furred wives and a gold claim on the Sixes.

Last night there was a full moon.

Today on the slopes of Blanco purple asters signal the end of summer –

sand-colored grass, cow parsley gone to seed, an uncommonly warm wind.

Below the Fresnel eye of the lighthouse, the beach is welcoming, expansive.

Minus tide, like an obsequious waiter, bows out before us,

leaving sand laid with delicate arrangements of shells, seaweed,

and silvered driftwood flushed downstream by the Sixes.

Along this beach, seals, or sometimes an otter, follow our movements.

Upright in the water, dark eyed, curious, the creatures look almost human.

Observe, on this apparently uninhabited stretch of sand,

we find cunning houses built of driftwood,

each a perfect, inviting shelter but empty as if created by spirits

who live, like the Irish Sidhe, invisible in wind and fog.

They tempt one to stay and not go back across the mountains,

but those who never left are buried here in the old Irish graveyard.

There is a chapel in the vacated house

Of the Catholic family who once lived here.

They logged and ran livestock in the marshy valley.

You might call it a spiritual place, or place of spirits

On this very beach Bigfoot tracks appeared one year,

And a man dredging the river met Bigfoot numerous times,

a large figure minding its own business. Others said:

orange, glowing eyes were seen, uncanny noises were heard,

trees were ripped from their roots and twisted like braids of schoolgirls.

We use the passive, to not claim too much.

Some say a mermaid lives in the river, but I have never seen her myself

so I have my doubts.

A few miles south is Battle Rock

where once an early expedition camped with a cannon.

Natives, possibly hostile, came to meet them. The white men fired.

Then retaliation. Many were killed on both sides.

Survivors told of a white man in a red shirt —

no one knew who he was but he came with the Indians.

Yet when the fight ended, as they left, the natives

kicked the body of the man in the red shirt as it floated near shore.

The settlers changed their plans and went north.

Sometimes among the scant and wind-bent trees on Battle Rock

people see a glimpse of red homespun, but climbing the steep path

they find nothing.

I've got more stories. Tomorrow, let's walk

the south side of Blanco to the Elk River,

and hike the trail through the bogs at Blacklock.

Or if you prefer, we'll hike up Humbug Mountain.

It's steep but rewarding. Some soldiers once go lost there.

That's why they call it Humbug.

SUCH A LUCKY ONE

Gary Carter – Port Orford

When I get to feeling blue
  Down to the beach I go
My backpack on
My cane in hand
  My litter bag in tow

On a log I shed my shoes
  And search among the rocks
Where I gather lots of things
Including bits of plastic, broken toys
  And, today, someone's shredded socks

Beer cans, bottles, cigarette lighters
  Broken glass that glitters
Someone's crusty shoes and a rusted toaster
That somehow washed ashore
  All these go in my bag of litter

Into my backpack goes
  Seashells, driftwood, some multi-colored stones

A frayed, purple rope, agates, Someone's lost hat

A Japanese float, an old glass ball
  And a good-sized critter's bleached out bone

But that's not all I find
  As I stroll along the shore

My soul absorbs unbounded beauty

Endless, romantic vistas, solitude, serenity, joy,
  Wonder, awe and a whole lot more

With both bags full I head for home
  Peace of mind restored

And thank the powers that be

That I am such a lucky one to have
  The sea at my back door

OREGON RAIN

Ron Staten - Bandon

I need the rain like a ripening field of grass hay does. I need rain to thrive
and grow just as the Douglas fir seedlings do that are three years old now up on
Morrison Ridge.

I've heard that every drop of rain carries a grain of sand all the way to the sea.
Learn to love the rain. Be a grain of sand and let it wash you away to your place by
the sea.

After the rain has stopped, I search the sides of ridges to find a seep: the
birthing place of rain from the earth. Know the way of water, and know the way of
life. From seep to rivulet to runnel to creek to river to sea. Learn to love water.

I know the birth place of Johnson Creek on Morrison Ridge where it seeps
out of the ground under a Spruce tree. This beginning place of a three-mile rush
to the sea is very tranquil. It's a secret place full of mystery where the boughs reach
to the ground all around. Only God and I know the birth place of Johnson Creek.

I COME TO THE SEA TO BE HEALED

Teresa Bird – Port Orford

The wind whips around my body

And the cold and salt sting my eyes, and my bones,

And my ears are filled with the roar of the waves

'til I can hardly think

   and hardly see, and hardly breathe,

and I am beat down and weary and I know

I am nothing

I huddle myself into the cleft of a rock

and wait to be swallowed

The rock whispers – "open your eyes, little one,

you are still alive."

And I see that it is true

BEFORE THE SQUALL

Alexandra Schiller - Winston

We walked together silently, hand in hand
Our steps imprinting in the wet, cloying sand
        -- A stroll before lunch.

Their sea-chiseled tops high above our shoulders
We mushed past mammoth gray-toned boulders
        -- Standing in a bunch

Breath-taking, chilly wind might have deterred us
But we knew that here they are ubiquitous
        -- "Mariah" packs a punch.

Rushing through time-worn crevices and caves
Constant the eternal, roaring ocean waves
        -- Slopping slunch, slunch, slunch.

Overhead. dark and threatening, banks of clouds
Raced as unrestrainable as rebellious crowds
        -- Rainfall a strong hunch.

Upon slimy seaweed we cruelly trod

Popping every slippery, ballooning pod

                     -- Just to feel the crunch.

Laughing like young children or crazy fools

We splashed our way through foamy tidal pools

                     -- Where tiny critters munch.

When sea gulls taunted, we tossed them crumbs

That sunless morning we played beach bums.

ROLLING INTO PORT ORFORD IN NOVEMBER

Tom West – Astoria and Portland, Oregon

I rolled into Port Orford after suffering a psychic dehydration in the big city. It was raining. Rain was moving across the highway like a phalanx. I caught the Port Orford radio station. Barry White was crooning about ecstasy. Never before in the history of Oregon had a small coastal town, rain and Barry White converged quite like this. I was ecstatic. I found a coffee shop and went inside. No one was there except the owner. I was cashless. He said I could pay later. I read the Port Orford newspaper. Top story: the liquor store had new winter hours and a new liquor store dog. I finished my coffee and went over to meet the dog. I did. I bought a pint of Wild Turkey from him and patted his head. Good whiskey dog! Pitch's Tavern next. I was the only one there except the bartender. I ordered a shot of rain with a dark beer chaser. I read the newspaper again. There was a column by an old man about driving his wife from Elk River to the Rogue River and back. He drove the long way, over rock-and-roll logging roads, deep into the watersheds. It took four hours. It was a date of some kind. I also read about a book of poems and short stories being published about the southern Oregon coast. Submissions were welcome. I started writing mine up on a Keno card with a golf pencil. The pot shop across the street was next. It was closed. The sign read they'd be right back. Sure they would. I knew where they were: at Battle Rock, relaxing, perhaps building a driftwood fort on the beach. I walked around town. I saw empty houses I wanted to occupy, rehabilitate. I saw a beautiful woman riding a bicycle. I wanted to move to Port Orford. I could walk to the beach, a liquor store, a pot shop, a coffee shop, a fish shop, a library, a greasy spoon, a thrift store, an organic food store, art galleries, a bar, a conservation outfit, a hardware store, past a building where Jack London once wrote a novel, and it would take thirty minutes. That's what I want in my life. I'm moving to Port Orford.

WHAT I LOVE ABOUT THE SOUTHERN OREGON COAST

Cathy Duckham - Bandon

I don't know what I like the most about this coast

It seems to put my mind in a relaxed Drain

And I don't mean the town

It means I live in lost and found . . .

Please tell me where I put my glasses down!

We go to the jetty to watch the waves

We go north to view the Sea Lion Caves

I love driving 101 admiring the cranberry bogs

Not caring if I slow down the trucks bearing logs.

I love living in a small town where everyone knows your name

And knows if one is crazy or just mildly insane

Instead of sitting in traffic delays

We are on the beach watching seals play.

Rush hour here is our cocktail hour

Can I please have another Pisco Sour?

I'm happy Drs. call us to remind us of appointments

They know being retired our days are disjointed

We love crabbing off Weber's pier

And having Toby's Crab Shack cook the little dears

Edgewater's is my favorite place to eat

Viewing the river from a prime window seat

Our library here in Bandon is the very best

Giving the ones in the cities a courtesy test

Being able to spend my life by the ocean

Fills my heart with emotion

I live my home here in paradise

And hope to live here until I die.

PACIFIC HEARTBEAT

Sandy Westerman – Port Orford

Pacific heartbeat.

Rhythm under coastal life.

Audible at night.

ELK RIVER ROAD

Therese Menzel – Elk River

We are Elk River Rats

A little of this and that

First few miles not like the next

With millhouses and meth houses, hexed

That are different from ranches

And cabins surrounded by branches

That are different from fancy homes

With stained glass and roster combs.

Old timers, part timers, full timers

All got the road down pat.

Fishermen, campers, grimers

Toss garbage where they're at

A few of us river rats

Clean up after these rude shats

.

Visitors walk the Elk River Hatchery

To view the start of the fish catchery.

Microcosm of rural Oregon

A little of this and that.

A pristine river where coexist the tame and the wild cat.

FATHER PETER DALLY

Frank Smith – Port Orford

He came to the South Coast a very young man
Fresh from Seminary with love and a zest for life
Newly ordained, anxious to start his career
As a saver of souls set to beat all strife

He was a large man, dark and straight, tall and sure
He had a winning smile and eyes a-sparkling
He had a soft voice yet easy to listen to
And a personality ever so pleasing

To some he was seen as a leader of the young
To some he was the Priest and man in command
To others he was the leader of the church
To most he was envisioned a giant among man

He organized the children, youth and adults
In the church, study, play and in fellowship
We all had a good place to fit in and learn
Not only about God and Christ but friendship

He took the youth out on many an outing

We swam, boated and played and had lots of fun

Up the rivers, on the shore or the lake

We learned about our Christ while playing in the sun

He taught us to think with our brain and our heart

He taught us how to reason and play chess

He taught us to be kind and help each other

He taught us belief in Christ and nothing less

He was a most prominent man in my life

Teaching me to believe in the heavens above

And our Father, Christ and the Holy Ghost

Also kindness, charity, faith, hope and love

Father Dally is in a great place today

He's not in pain and has no furrow to plod

He is sitting with the Angels and the Saints

In Company of the Spirit, Christ and God

In honor of Father Peter Dally

JUST GIVE ME THE INTEL, MAN

A future conversation with my year-and-a-half old son.

Tim Scahill - Bandon

The sand spilled into his shoe from the back. He HATES it when that happens. He felt the sharp pokes into his leg as he walked. The beach grass stabbing his leg was an all too familiar feeling. There will be little blood speckles on the inside of his jeans.

He turned to the boy who was trailing behind. "You comin'?" he asked jokingly.

"Yeah. Chill out dad!" he replied.

They plopped down on a giant tree trunk that the ocean had clumsily, yet gracefully, tossed onto the beach a few weeks back. It had become their favorite spot.

His son wasted no time. "What did you want to be when you grew up when you were my age?"

"Well, the list was quite long, and you're not ready," he said with a little smirk, knowing full well he was going to launch into "dad advice mode" and savor every second.

"I know what you're doing! Just give me the intel, man!" his son chanted, knowing this game, but allowing himself to fall for his father's dumb bit.

18

"Okay, okay," he started. "First, I wanted to be a chef. I loved baking and looking up recipes with your grandma. My favorite thing was to bake a cake that looked like hamburger."

He continued. "Then, I wanted to sing. I joined some select local choirs and sang at church. I even sang in the barbershop choir!

"After that a musician. I made some friends in college, and we started a band! We toured the country playing houses, small venues and crashing on couches. We even got signed to a local label. Next a photographer and videographer. I used to make movies, edited clips for classes and made video skits with friends.

"Next a graphic designer who helps make the world a more beautiful place while telling a story. Eventually, I wondered how I could do all of these things. So, I got an internship and made websites for anyone who would let me. Now, that's how we can afford to feed you! Well, I guess I barely can afford to feed you since you're eating us out of house and home."

There was a long silence. My joke went ignored as usual. The ocean churned. They marveled at its graceful power, thinking about the unending life choices in front of his son.

He interrupted the ocean's pitch-perfect song. "Can I tell you a secret?" he asked, letting the question hang for a moment, only half expecting an answer. "There is no better job than being your dad. Being right here, right now, with you . . . here at the edge of the country, talking about life."

The waves sang another verse. His son knew that his father was now expecting him to spill his most profound thoughts all over the beach, just as he had. He finally spoke.

"Being a musician sounds way easier than all that other stuff."

FOGHORN

Patrick Shuff – Coos Bay

Matter into matters bye it's good and gone

Maddened into madder spurred moment into dawn

High speed chase down dead-end alley: crawling into the bog

Koosbay organ: Kafkaesque horn casting coasts beneath the fog.

Don't want much from it no just an easy yawn

Mercy's mirror is missing took where giving all has gone

No sooner once begins clock spins its broken cog

Koosbay organ: Kafkaesque horn casting coasts beneath the fog.

Echoing stardust twinkly eyes skies deep caverns borne in tides

Diary of songs once sung bobbing on the sea of sighs

Surf crashes onto shores of refuse: here's the abandoned log

Koosbay organ: Kafkaesque horn casting coasts beneath the fog.

A SEA OF POSSIBILITY

Linda Marchand - Bandon

The Bandon surf is pounding
It envelopes my ears
Coming in, receding out
Just like the growing years.

Within a quarter century
I've walked along these shores
Mostly when it's sunny
And sometimes when it pours.

The sea is ever changing
Each visit something new
It gives me fresh perspective
For my life, another view

Wild waves come rushing in
During crispy winter storms
They crash and break upon the rocks
Sometimes a rainbow forms.

It seems my life is rushing past

And I'm being broken too

The rainbow holds a promise

That there's still much I can do.

I sense I'm at a turning point

What can my future be?

Ions dance in an atmosphere

Of possibility

Light reflecting on the surface

Leads toward the horizon

And vanishing beyond that point

I see my future lies in.

BEAUTIFUL BANDON BY THE
SEA (B.B.B.T.S.)

Colette Fuchs – Bandon

Pinch me! I live in a place surrounded by sounds I love. The rain beating on the rooftop, the wind whistling in the trees and the roar of the Pacific Ocean. Living on the southern Oregon coast is a dream come true.

In 2007 I got married for the second time. I debated whether to continue to work or not. I chose the "or not' option. Our first endeavor as a couple was to search for a writer's cabin. A place for us to get away. I was looking for a place to write. My goal in retirement was to pursue a freelance writing career. The cabin would be a peaceful place to relax, write and enjoy our dogs. So we built our "cabin" along the southern Oregon coast, near B.B.B.T.S.

I expect the unexpected in terms of weather here. The breezes blow almost daily. It can be dark and raining when I gaze out the window, then, as if by magic, the sun bursts out, and it's as if those rain clouds I saw earlier never existed. It's remarkable. Change is the spice of life. The weather changes provide daily spice.

The top of my list of personal favorites is our shoreline and the impressive ocean views. The beaches are simply exquisite. There are many other beautiful beaches in this world. I've seen many in Florida, California, as well as along the Australian and New Zealand coastlines. But Bandon beaches are spectacular. Just stunning. Unlike any other beaches I have viewed. I think the numerous sea stacks generate a lot of the beauty of our shoreline. Waves that crash on and around them provide a daily show for us.

The south coast has a wide variety of trees and wildlife. We have sea lions on the rocks in among the sea stacks close to shore. (We also hear the hungry roar of a real lion from the game park south of us.) We have whales migrating right off our shoreline, adding occasional water spouts to our views in December and March when the gray whales migrate.

I enjoy my little "neck of the woods". My former home was located in northern Oregon, where the sun didn't come out to shine much, often for weeks at a time. I am glad to have discovered the southern Oregon coast for myself. Peaceful, enjoyable, plenty of sun along with the rain and I **AM LOVING** it.

DAWNWATCH

Jeanne Gammell – Gold Beach

Too soon my November days draw down and early risings bring long

watches for the sunrise. At the river-bend a gravel bar reaches stony fingers

toward the current, seeking the black river's channel.

Someone – something – ghosts along the bank: amorphous, silent,

insubstantial, and is gone. The last stars, dawnwatching with me, like Bedouins,

have decamped.

Nights' candles snuffed out one by one, as the hill up-east limns a conifer –

dark silhouette against a pale pearling on the horizon.

The black river rolls and riffles with a moire' sheen, gleaming under the

Lightening dawn as a brushstroke of golden pink tints an abalone cloud above the

hill.

My mug of coffee cools. My hands ae cold.

The south shore autumn foliage glows yellow like a dozen peeking suns

as Earth's sun spills across the hill and gilds the river pools.

It is morning on the Rogue River.

It is a mid-November dawn.

OUR BLISSFUL COASTAL MOTHER

David Woof – Oregon Wild Rivers South Coast

Cooling silken mist – fills

salty coastal air.

Low clouds – churn

where rising fog ends.

A moist uterine

cocoon of renewal.

After rainless summer

we tasted smoke – in each

spoken word.

Smoke that shaded – and cooled

wild salmon rivers.

Wild fire cleansed the land.

High drifting soot –

Hastened rain – bringing

Forth renewed browse,

And cover for our wild things.

The fecund womb – of our coastal mother

where sea, fog, winds,

Fire, rain, and sun — rise and settle
in ancient rhythms of renewal.

GOING

Lily Mars – Langlois

With cries
of joy
not terror
the geese go
noisily south
in October
calling out
their warning

a strong sharp signal to
our off-kilter brains
our estranged hearts
our somehow still
open spirits'

while we may go
on in silence
or regret
the geese go

with exuberance

more forward than gone

they fly together

year after year

with their

cries

CURRY COUNTY

Frances Holmstrom — 1881–1956 — North Bend and Harbor[1]

Curry County, you who sit

With your back to the world, disdaining it

`With your back to the world and your feet in the sea

Reading its riddles endlessly —

Curry County, you who wear

Nest of Eagles in your hair,

Who bind your forests with golden streams,

Hiding treasure for miners' dreams,

Who wear white bones of the sunken hosts

In a cruel necklace about your coasts:

To whom the sea-gulls cry is a song

Tuned to the breakers your shores along:

You who clasp to your jealous breast

The last frontier of the fading west -

Curry County, do you know

---

[1] Submitted by Helen Picca

A lover leaves you when I go?

And if it happens I die some day,

A friend, let his name be what it may,

So that he loves both thee and me,

Shall seek some height that is part of thee:

Cooley's Point or Battle rock,

Or some unnamed ledge where the seabirds flock,

Shall take up a pebble and fling it down

Into the caldron whose angers drown

The sound of it falling, and as it drops

The wind shall chant thro the torn tree tops,

Curry, Curry, beside they shore

Hold thou this memory evermore

BACK IN TIME

Helen Picca – Port Orford

When I saw the sign for the park up ahead I told Jack to pull in. He looked at me like I was insane and said, "You're kidding, right?"

I assured him I was not and told him it was a special place that he would not believe until he saw it. So, we pulled into Prehistoric Gardens and parked. There were only a few cars in the lot, which made me glad as we would have the place pretty much to ourselves.

"Jen, I love you, but don't you think this is a little hokey? Looking at a bunch of plastic dinosaurs?"

"It's so much more than dinosaurs, and besides, they're not plastic. Come on. I guarantee you will love it." He acquiesced and we got out of the car.

I explained to Jack that this place had opened in 1955 with about a dozen replicas, which is when I had first come. Amy was about two and I had pushed her in a stroller while the others ran around oohing and aahing and shrieking with glee. The man who created it had been a CPA from back east, but was also a sculptor. He moved his family to southern Oregon in search of the perfect place for his park and found the prehistoric rainforest. Over the course of 30 years he created 23 sculptures, which are steel frames covered by cement, then meticulously hand-painted.

Greeting us at the trailhead was a Tyrannosaurus Rex, one of the most recognizable and scariest of creatures. This was followed by the largest, a Brachiosaurus which is 86 feet long and 46 feet tall, and took four years to create. It is spellbinding to stand next to the creature, looking at its huge feet and green hide as you crane your neck up to see its head. It is huge.

We followed the path and little by little were drawn into the ancient rainforest. It was misting, only adding to the mysteriousness of the place. At each turn there was a prehistoric reptile lurking, taking us further back into time. It was silent and eerie and so moist, every surface dampened by mist. We forgot about our daily lives and were plunged back to a time when only plants, trees and dinosaurs roamed the earth - it was magical. I looked up at Jack and he looked at me, both of us feeling lost in time. All that moved was the rain dripping of the leaves and ferns of this primitive rainforest. He drew me to him and kissed me in the most tender, loving way. Time stopped . . . in that instant, there was only he and I on the whole planet. Our spell was broken by the sound of a child shrieking at the sight of the T-Rex. We broke from the kiss but continued to gaze into each other's eyes. He whispered "Thank you" into my ear and I knew he felt the serenity of the forest and that all the nonsense of our daily lives ceased to exist.

We continued on the path discovering and admiring the authenticity and workmanship of these incredible statues, and the raw natural beauty by which we were surrounded, until all too soon we were back at the car. "Thank you" he said again. "I feel so light and free. What a magical place . . . one I would have surely missed if not for you."

GREEN AND PLEASANT LANDS

Patricia Huntzinger – Port Oford

A vertical land, of water and
Gothic green cathedrals pointing skywards,
Tethered to the earth by rain in slanting lines.
Rain, which, in its immensity, mocks the mild
Damp days of England

Here, although we count the engauged inches and exclaim,
Nature is immeasurable, untranslatable in any
Language that I know; like the sounds of unfamiliar birds
Whose calls are strange and disconnected
From the creatures who feed beyond our windows.

Here there are no songs to lead my thoughts
Back to England, but only sounds which make no sense
To my ignorant, uneducated ear.
This new landscape has become my home
And I must learn to speak its language.

Here, among the water and the trees,

The latitude and longitude of our world.

We move and breathe and share our home and yet

My home for more than fifty years lies in waiting

To trip me in a heart-stopping fall

Which, unlike those in dreams, remains

By day to taunt my wakefulness.

Here, I tether myself to you; lines of intricate intimacy holding me

On course when blinded by water, lost in trees.

Lines of communication unspoken, felt deep in the heart's core.

Here, landscapes of the soul require no translation

Here, the water and the trees blend and blind

Here, I find my song and the music which combines

My Oregon, my England.

Here is home, where you are.

OREGON WOMAN

James Huntzinger – Port Orford

Ava Thompson was born in the early 20th century at Lost River Dam, which makes her about as Oregonian as you can get. The greater portion of her 80+ years was lived on the coast, its cities and her preferred rural communities. From early in her adult married years, as 'Bertie' Satterlee, she was a merchant – buying, selling, bidding, speculating, gaining, losing. When I was five years old, I had my first glimpse of the Oregon coast when my father brought me along to visit Ava, his sister. She then owned and operated Davy Jones's Locker in Charleston (should a store be named for a Welsh keeper of drowned sailors, in a fishermen's community?.......discuss) We stayed in rooms upstairs of the large old building. She had then, and invariably kept thereafter, a black Labrador Retriever and a black cat.

My Aunt bought, or traded, for stores and restaurants all along the coast from Reedsport to Harbor. She never considered so much as a bare acre on the California side, keeping firm and definite opinions about state and local governments all of her life. She disparaged big government and big business. Two of her maxims; If you have to incorporate, somebody else'll be wearing your britches, and a First Principle: Get up in the morning. She supported small business and Cooperatives, and was well known for grub-staking: advancing capital to individuals who demonstrated gumption and a valid business plan. Allegedly, recompense always turned up. She had an instinctive altruism, a natural empathy for people deserving it, antipathy toward those who did not.

She maintained and shared strong opinions, but never strong language or drink – she was a devout Christian all of her life. God would eventually punish any and all scoundrels; his Son helped look after the kids. I admired some of her particular skills: she could arbitrate at family or civil feuds; she was a whiz at fly-casting, and a dependable water diviner who 'witched wells' with green twigs from any tree and she could turn the devastating angst of teens' years to an enabling sense of value and contentment.

Visitors were welcomed to any of her consecutive 'shops' in Gold Beach, Port Orford, Bandon and Brookings, with occasional forays inland, to Mohawk, for instance, and Powers (arguably a coastal city whenever there is a little help from the river's winter floods). In Port Orford she owned and operated the Paradise Café, making her own, famous pies and offering plain American cooking with no radical surprises except corn fritters, which for a while provided an alternative to hash browns.

Ava considered herself a pioneer woman: sufficient, proficient, practical, capable, and confident. She had red hair that she didn't fuss about, and a good aim with a rifle, hatchet or filleting knife. I believe most Oregon Women maintain her stamp: Stand up and speak out. Speak up and stand out. Oregoniennes: I see them all around me.

THRIVING HERE

Cairehn McGowan – Port Orford

The roar of smells, the rush of

memories

another's sense of loss

is my treasure

Seaweed, tossed careless on the beach,

hides collectible shells.

Home – where our senses

Are invigorated, loved, saved

While the firs stand tall

spectacular

immune to wind and rain

the beaches, ravaged and lovely

but my senses demand more

thriving here

And are fed by the constant

Uproar

MY SANCTUARY TO
YESTERDAY

Nancy Wright – San Tan Valley, Arizona

Dear Port Orford,

They say that "Beauty is in the eye of the beholder". Thirty years ago I found Port Orford and know what true beauty is.

Every year I travel back to walk the beautiful beaches and smell the fresh air of the ocean.

Just being in this quiet town brings peace to my soul. For me, it's as if I have walked into yesterday.

Everyone I have met here lives and works in Port Orford because they feel the draw into serenity and unity with their fellow man.

After all these years, the scenic views of the light houses, cliffs and forests, remind me of a hand painted work of art.

Every time I close my eyes and remember the smell of the pine trees and the spray of the ocean on my face, I am once again at peace with the world.

Today is yesterday's tomorrow. If I am fortunate enough, I will once again journey back into time and once again find peace in the town a few call home.

I have come to know poets and artists that have lived in Port Orford for many years. Even though they travel the United States and beyond, the draw to this town is very strong.

Although it's just a spot on the map, I have come to call it my home away from home.

I have traveled the entire length and breadth of the United States and Canada and still feel the pull to Port Orford.

There is true beauty in what God has created and I have found it here.

NOBILITY AT REST

Lurell Bailey – Port Orford

There's something 'bout a shipwreck
That takes hold upon my heart
Sunken deep in ocean bottoms-
Or broken on the shoals apart.

For they all begin so regal,
Heading out to seas unknown
And the men that serve as sailors
Sometimes never make it home.

And some they carried treasure
Coins of silver, jewels and gold-
Then some vessels made for fishing
Often sailing forth so bold.

But the sea's a mighty terror
With tempests showing rage
For no reason known, she sinks them
Breaks them rough as on a stage.

Often stories go down with them
The 'why' is never seen
And the men who manned those beauties
Are remembered strong and lean.

A reprieve is sometimes given
Such as with the Jamie T-
When she foundered on Cape Blanco reef
Wounded, sat there on the sea.

For her power sources failed
Four brave hearts began to fail
They put on their survival suits
And made that Coastguard call.

And they felt the salt spray hit them
As they hit rocks nearby
Soon they heard the Coastguard coming
Beating hard across the sky.

The winds beat at the them lusty
But one strong man braved the foam-

Calmed the men and swam them shoreward

And brought them safely home.

There's something 'bout a shipwreck

Where men had never trod

That reminds us, Oh so often

That our lives depend on God.

BATTLE ROCK EXPERIENCES

Sharon Lovie — Port Orford

In October of 1952, after divorcing our stepfather, Mamma moved us from Ophir, Oregon to Port Orford, Oregon to begin our new lives. I was ten years old at the time. My older brother Lloyd and I were buddies. We were always up for new adventures.

On weekends, Lloyd and I spent time exploring Battle Rock. Battle Rock sat on the beach at the edge of town. There were indentations in the rock that were footholds to climb up the face and onto the top of the rock. Back in the olden days, there had been a famous battle on the rock, and a grave was up there, it was one of the men that had been part of the battle. There were trees on top and greenery. There was also a lot of poison oak on the rock. A path led down through the middle of the foliage to the ocean side of the rock. There we would sit as the waves crashed against the rock, tossing spray into the air.

Down on the beach, when the tide was low, we could see the tunnel that went clear through the rock. One day Lloyd and I were standing on the beach looking at the opening to the tunnel. "Suzy, let's go through the tunnel. The tide's low, we can do it."

"But, Lloyd, what if a big wave comes?"

"It'll be okay. No waves that big will come when the tide is out. Come on, let's do it!"

"Okay." I always trusted Lloyd; he knew everything. So, we waded in. The water was up to the middle of our calves. We got almost to the middle of the cave when the wave came. The water level started rising to my knees, my waist. "Lloyd, it's getting too deep. I'm scared."

Suddenly Lloyd yelled: "Turn around and run! Faster—Faster—Hurry!" By the time we got out of the cave the water was up to my neck! It was all I could do to keep from floating, and I couldn't swim. The water had reached Lloyd's armpits as he reached out and grabbed me, pulling me to safety. Lloyd's eyes were as big as mine. He had been afraid, too.

"Let's never do that again," Lloyd's voice quivered. "It just isn't safe."

We never told Mamma what we had done. We didn't want her to worry.

NUTRIA (COYPU)

Susan Vineyard – Coos Bay

I heard a local farmer say,
"Them Argentines are here to stay!"

They came by ship back in the days
of Lewis and Clark – The big fur craze

With beaver face and rat-like tail,
their rodent pelts were made for sale

While farmed for coats and hats and capes,
They seized a moment to escape

They scattered at the river's mouth
And sprawled from Tillamook County south

Tunneling farms and fields of grain,
Devouring crops – They're such a pain!

They bare orange fangs, and grunt like pigs,

and make the water's edge their digs

So watch out when you're walking dogs
Along the wetlands, sloughs, and bogs

They just might come across your path
and waddle to a mossy bath

Nutria are here to stay-
twenty-pound rodents right here in Coos Bay!

MUSHROOMS

Cher Sides - Bandon

Gifts of the rain,

anticipated,

yet still they surprise.

Show-offs, they are,

that demand pauses

in my forest ramblings:

scarlet clowns sporting polka dots;

queenly fluted chanterelles;

gnarled lobsters in ruddy eruptions;

sooty gnomish elfin saddles;

tiny translucent fairies;

delicate coral spires;

carmine tribes of witches' hats:

curving purple trumpets;

turkey tails feathering a rotted trunk;

rubbery orange peel gummies;

beefy boletes tempting a feast;

And more---many more,

each emerging in their turns.

So like those

urgent poems that

spring up

overnight,

but only in their seasons.

HARP OF THE WINDS

Teressa K. – Port Orford

In the land of the Qua-To-Mah long before the pale faces came,

There lived an ancient people who were proud, fierce and brave.

Happily they fished and hunted in prime-evil forests evergreen

That grew to the singing shores of a mighty ocean, frothy, clear and clean.

Gone are the giant fir forests and its handsome natives within.

They were sent to distant sands that held not the spirits of these Indians.

Autumn through summer they're no more. For what's left of these native bands

Are barren, howling hills and shores and keening of the Harp-of-the Winds

On the last warm winds of summer braves fly south on feathered feet.

Heeding the call of their ancestors' beat-beat-beat.

Soaring and gliding like tree-men along boughs bouncing in the breeze

Their hearts hum-humming with wind harp strumming spirits of the trees

Oh-ee-ay-ee-ay-ee-oh-oh-ee-ay-ee-ay. Heh.

COASTAL BLESSINGS

Martha Schram – Langlois

Spring wrings waning clouds

out fall foxglove, lupine, blackberry

fir, hemlock, pine

juncos and robins return

speckling grassy places

to listen for dinner rising

Summer deer drink life from

creeks, streams and ponds

frogs sing from puddles

wetness pools, hillside blossoms

welcome bumbling visitors

new lives emerge from hidden places

Autumn dries seeds

with north winds to fly

them to new ground

all is poised, waiting

a return to rain changing

brown to green again

Winter clouds weep for joy
They reach down to kiss
blessing with promise of life
this ground is a sponge
digesting, integrating, opening
to hibernal tears

RECIPES FROM THE WILD ROGUE[2]

David Kunde – Gold Beach –"The Wandering Star"

Recipes from the Wild Rogue contain the ingredients for great food. When brought together in the right amounts they make a dish we savor, a dish we share, and will often make again.

For many of us the Rogue River Wilderness area shares much of the same results. When making a dish every ingredient has its own texture, its own smell and its own taste. When placed together in the right amount we have a "WOW" factor. The Rogue River has that, the nano-second you step into it. It's a lot like that pastry shop. Open the door, begin to walk in, and WOW! you just have to have something.

When I got out of my car the first time I took a step into the environment of the Rogue. I felt the firmness of the ground, stood and watched the flow of the river, took a deep breath of the sweetness – from its firs, cedars, myrtle woods and eucalyptus – then I turned and noticed the flowers in bloom, the hummingbirds, seagulls, blue-jays, hawks and eagles. I became spell-bound. All these became just the right ingredients, in just the right amounts, for you and me to smell, to feel, to savor – THIS is my pastry shop, and non-fattening! Not a sugar high; a nature high. This is the true recipe of the Rogue.

---

[2] Authors note: Originally written as the introduction to the website "Recipes from the Wild Rogue".

WOOD THRUSH

AJ Darrel – Port Orford

Sitting alone on a bench by the sea

Listening to waves as they crash into rocks

There are tall, orange flowers by a memorial

In front of which I sit quietly

Thinking thoughts that are my own

As I breathe in the sweet air

I am pulled away from my reflections

by the chatter of a small bird

While she enjoys the nectar of a flower

I reach for my camera

She then sits atop a bloom

providing a perfect pose

After I snap the photo,

She turns her head towards me

as if to say, "Farewell"

then, swiftly flys away

Smiling contently I look at the ocean

and cannot remember there ever having been

a more pleasant Memorial Day

ODE TO THE BLACKBERRY

By Jan Dacayana — Port Orford — 1935-2004[3]

Cold rain drips from the thorny vines

Tugging at clothes and skin

Nude of leaves like giant webs

Waiting to pull you in

How could God give us such a plant

So ugly and so bold

It grows so fast no fence or flower

Can fight its choking hold

You cut, you chop, and whack all day

Dried blood on hands and clothes

How could God give us such a wicked plant

That makes so many woes

And as the days grow longer, and spring arrives

The vines begin to wander, leaf out and thrive

---

[3] Submitted by daughter Lani Martin — Gold Beach

More dangerous now with hidden thorns

That attack if you get near

How could God give us such a sneaky plant

That grabs you from the rear

Armed with ladders and long-sleeved shirts

Reaching for berries 'neath leafy skirts

Buckets full, we beat, retreat

To pots waiting on the stove

Where black juice bubbling and sugar sweet

Is stirred with pride and love

Faces glow, savoring the victorious sight

Of filled crystal jars, lids screwed on tight

Standing in regimental lines, as if to say

"Hail, Oh conquerors of the vines, your battle won today."

Then on a cold and wintry morn

When toast and jam you serve

You'll know why God gave us such a pesky, thorn-filled plant

It's more than we deserve!

WHERE ARE WE?

Jennifer Wilson — Port Orford

We stopped at the
  "Ocean View"
Like castaways do
  To see the sea
And our future too

Our boat would be safe
  Up on the dock
With a jetty to protect us
  When the weather was rough

Landmarks like Humbug
  To guide our navigation
And Cape Blanco's lighthouse
  Silently saying . . .
"Go south little dingy."

THE LOGGER

Carolyn Prola —Myrtle Point

With his chain saw he spends his time,

Cutting down the Pondersa Pine

His cutting logs don't have large leaves,

His hickory shirts get shorter sleeves.

BLANCO BLUE

Ava Richey — Bandon

Sky's morning blush
pale sun aloft
Clouds build and rise
above enveloping fog

A narrowing comes of
temperature and light
It's much less than day
Seems almost like night

Gray days leave moist
cheek-kissed greetings
and a glow from the nip
of cold breezes retreating

Thunder and crashing surf
meet in a rumbling refrain
Don't count on a view
until after the rain

Pungence of sea life
salty tang on the tongue
bring summer memories
of kids and dogs having fun

Some folks are saddened
by the ambiance of winter
Others find exhilaration
In this coastal splendor

HOW IS A CALIFORNIA GIRL LIKE A HIMALAYAN BLACKERRY?

Erin Scott – Port Orford

She is sweet

but sour if picked

too soon. Wait

until summer sun

has ripened her fruit.

she is strong

heart-y

and delicious.

Still, Native

Orgonians

judge:

She is an invasive

species.

BROOKINGS – MY GREAT EXPECTATIONS

John Canalin – Brookings

I expected clean

And robust ocean breezes,

but am exhilarated by the swell

with each sweet breath

that I faithfully expel.

I expected green and wooded landscapes

that diverge on the rocky surf of blue,

but am envious of

the harmony that

this diversity imbues

I expected a cool congeniality

amidst the hard-working community

and the infiltrating seekers of leisure,

but am heartened by the genuine

and random acts of kindness

and this makes my heart a believer.

I expected to leave the big city blues

for the serenity of frequent pause,

but am impressed for achieving

much, much more,

Strong body and mind with hopeful cause.

She steels my strength,

Secures my senses,

And sustains my spirit and soul.

(And of course, fresh fish and crab!!)

WHERE THE EAGLE FLIES

Shirley Richards – Coos Bay

It's beautiful here
  Where the Eagle flies
Clear and blue
  No sadness, no sorrow

It's beautiful here where the eagle flies
  He soars with grace, gliding in the wind
High and free where he loves to be
  His wings spread wide soaring in the sun

The Eagle, the Angels and Me

EWAUNA[4]

Bill Cullenward — Port Orford

Rising

from ocean waters

silhouetted

against

crimson-gold

of

setting sun

quiet

in her own meaning

she waits,

teaches,

with silent whispers

beckons

thoughts

of wonder

---

[4] *Ewauna was the Native American name for Face Rock, a sea stack located off the coast of Bandon, Oregon. It is a wonderful legend.*

DISCOVERING BANDON

Annis Cassells

Early afternoon in July 1996, I rode into Old Towne Bandon on my candy apple red Goldwing and checked into the hostel. It faced the marina and the Coquille River, and the boats bobbed in the slight wind. I fell in love with this little town that day.

Bandon was a dot on the coastal map I'd never heard of until I spent the night in a California redwood hostel. Two young women were plotting their route and where they'd stop next. "Bandon has a hostel," one pointed out as she looked up from the hostel directory she held. Her traveling companion checked the map and noted Bandon was only a few hours' drive and might be a good place to stay. I made a mental note to stop there for a look.

After settling in I took off to the west on 1st Street then walked along the shoulder of the jetty road. That's where the stunning Coquille River Lighthouse came into view through the tall grasses that grew by the roadside. Four years later, a photo I took of that lighthouse kept me grounded and calm as I glanced at it from time to time while writing my Master's Exam.

And I walked to the beach—a beach like none other—with its unique, spectacular rock formations and the distant call of the foghorn. I ambled along, collecting stones for at least a mile before backtracking to the hostel then exploring the town in search of a bowl of hot soup.

True, there have been many changes in Bandon since I first discovered it, but the town still maintains its friendly, homey feel, and a beach stroll still delights me. It's one of my favorite spots to spend time during my summer stay in Coos Bay.

When I ask returning visitors what they'd like to do, the answer is always, "I want to go to Bandon."

THE HILLS ARE ALIVE WITH
THE SOUND OF MUSIC

Dr. Grace Bonnell – Port Orford

Highway 101 had been enchanting for the past 50 miles. Tall majestic pines, of several kinds, stand tall, sometimes seeming to kiss the ocean along this winding road. Panoramic views of an aqua blue ocean and a rugged coast on the other side. It was breathtaking. A place where my love for trees and ocean were meeting. I felt something very special.

This place had a vibration that was vital and alive. I felt there must be history here that didn't meet the eye also. The businesses along the highway were small, privately owned and there was space, beautiful space with views of trees and ocean. These hills were alive with the sound of silence and beauty. As I traveled on I couldn't stop thinking of Port Orford, Oregon.

My trip had been carefully mapped out. After Seattle I would travel south toward home. I couldn't stop thinking or talking about that small town on the Southern Oregon Coast while in Seattle. As planned, I headed down Interstate 5 and at the junction in Roseburg, Oregon, I turned and headed for the coast. The Southern Oregon Coast was calling my name.

Arriving in Port Orford, I made a few stops to talk with folks and just drove around this town that has a unique vibration, among the antique stores, art galleries, restaurants, the large open harbor framed by a huge Seamount and fishing dock with cranes that lifted all the boats up nightly. Among the Hidden Treasures here, the Lighthouse and Museums add to the charm and vibration. Everywhere I turned I learned history. I actually put an offer on a property before continuing my travels south.

Two weeks later I returned. After that deal fell through I started my search for the perfect place. I felt more and more at home and continued to learn and be introduced to the writers, musicians and artists here also. After a couple of days of serious searching the realtor showed me a property in the woods five minutes above town. This was it!

Six months later here I was, finding more beauty and hidden treasures in the area and sixteen years later here I live on my little piece of heaven. My home in the pines and conifers and rhododendrons, planted by the first property owners, give me eleven different colors of glory each spring, plus my roses, and a garden space. Each morning I wake to beauty.

Here on the hill I enjoy the Sounds of Music on the wind singing in the trees and the Sound of Music of the waves on the sand. I can't see the ocean but I hear singing every day. Although it gets harder to travel the distance to a doctor, hospital or major shopping center (I'd rather shop online anyway) I'm forever grateful for my little piece of heaven in the woods and the peace of my Sounds of Music.

MY COMPASS POINTS SOUTH

Melinda Blegen — Brookings

Facing North,

The needle waivers,

I am not drawn by this direction.

Turning to the South,

I sense hope.

After 40 years of living someone else's dream,

I am free to choose my own way.

Moving Southward, drawn to the Pacific,

I find a little piece of paradise.

The sound of the surf calms me

From deep within.

As I gaze at the silently flowing Chetco,

a cormorant dives into the depths,

a sea lion rolls in the shallows,

a gull cries overhead and

I realize you offer no resistance.

I yearn to be more like you.

As my healing continues, I know

I am home, my compass pints South.

MOTHER NATURE
GRANDMOTHER MOON

Kristi Disbrow — Port Orford

Great Spirit nurtures the rivers and mountains,

all the oceans on planet earth.

Coral, greens, and lavender-blues

All are precious since time began

Mother Nature dances the oceans in my world.

Great Spirit gives me many treasures,

all the seeds that live within.

Reds, yellow, ebony-white

All are cultivated in the dirt

Mother Nature gives with flowers and trees in my world.

Great Spirit cherishes the many people,

All the children in this world.

Pinkie, greens, spicy-delight

All are given with love to you

Grandmother Moon dances with rain for you.

Great Spirit gives me peace of darkness

All the stars and bright moonlight.

Clouds of grey and foggy-dew

All are given bright sunlight

Grandmother Moon surely gives you rainbows too.

OREGON COAST RAIN

Michael Disbrow – Port Orford

A gust blows down rain from the trees

My first thought; that's poetry

Winter here on the Oregon coast

The mist floats by

Just like a ghost

Little rivulets flow through the chicken yard

Winter rains both soft and hard

COMING HOME

Jennifer Shook - Bandon

Steep cliff,

Massive rocks,

Scattered stones,

Smooth pebbles,

Soft sand,

I stumble in my haste to reach you.

Intimate joy awaits.

We touch,

Sudden cold,

I gasp with exhilaration,

A clandestine meeting,

Human feet,

Ocean water,

Push and pull of possessive waves.

Too soon our time is at an end,

    Will I remember you?

I try to memorize your music.

    Crescendo, fade......

        Crescendo fade ......

            Crescendo, fade......

THE OREGON DUNES

Jean Harris - Reedsport

Masses will come

    Not just to see

    Or to listen

    Or to conquer

    But out of curiosity

When they are here

    They will celebrate

    With nature, with earth

    With self, and the Creator

    And will anticipate

Coming Again

    Then to see

    And to hear

    Maybe to conquer

    And satisfy their curiosity.

They will share

      This awesome splendor

      With a friend

      Or a lover,

      Or a stranger

Feeling when

      They turn to leave

      God is Great

      Life is good

      Knowing they did receive

An experience

      They cannot express

      With words

      With pictures

      Only to self, they must confess

IN COOS COUNTY

Liesa Kister – Coos Bay

Mist draped verdant hills

Leaf, feather, needle, fur.

Discover paths

Toward undulating dunes.

Endless dance of tides,

bones revealed

Agates, driftwood, shell.

I am left

with a ripe berry smile

ONE LITTLE ACRE

Everett Olson – Bandon

Oregon is a special place for me and Phyllis. We discovered Oregon on one of our vacations and little did we know it was the place we would spend the rest of our lives. The abundant variety of green, the beauty of the coastal shoreline, was nothing like I had seen. Surely it is a piece of heaven on earth. As far as I was concerned it was the Garden of Eden at one time.

Being from Wisconsin and newly discharged from the service I saw Oregon as a place of contentment and beauty. We settled here and began a search for an acre of land we could build on. Most of the land for sale were hillsides where you would have to carve a level lot for a house. The search went on for a year.

We found 80 acres on a hillside, on a stream, but no bridge for access. Everything we looked at had a drawback. 15 acres on top of a hill, high price, and owners in no hurry to sell. As a last ditch effort, we put an ad in a small paper. We stated we were in search of an acre of land, and, lo and behold, we met the real treasure of Freda Stankavich. She was a widow and had 10 acres of flat land for sale. The deal was sweet and we never hesitated.

Freda's father-in-law had proved up 160 thru the Homestead Act and Freida had 80 acres she was slowly selling in parcels. We had originally wanted to buy one acre and build a shed. All of a sudden, we were buying 10 acres and building a cabin, a big jump.

Freda was a very down to earth person, no pretentions. She maintained about 10 acres of blueberries, with U-Pickers during the season. The first year on the land we were able to harvest cranberries.

Freda often had us over for dinner and always a board game after. She would talk about how her husband, Matt, and his brother invented the first dry picking machine for cranberries. Of course her favorite story was how she caught a 30 pound ling cod and out-fished her family and rubbed it in for years.

We met so many people who expressed a true kindness and concern I have never felt any other place. It was definitely our home for life. Friends would show up with a meal in hand just when we were short, delivering more than we could eat. The great resource we had were the people living in an amazing place surrounded by beauty and love.

BEACH WALK

Megan Maloney – Bandon

Sharp, salt air on skin

White noise of surf against sand
Soul released, at peace.

Young Writers of the Southern Oregon Coast

MEANING OF LIFE

Jennifer Himmelrich (age 13) - Harbor Lights Middle School – Bandon

As I walk through a vast long stretch of sand I could taste the salt in the air. Something was calling my name. As I look back I see a canvass that awaits. I see no one, just something. I see an array of rocks with many different colors as well as a beautiful ocean with an amazing background. It was a sunset of blue clouds with a vibrant pink peeking through. I could see through the horizon all the possibilities that await. Right then I knew to live in the moment, and in that moment I found the meaning of life, my purpose. My purpose was to be happy and to have peace in mind when I see something so beautiful. Something more than just beauty a meaning. Beauty is what you make it.

I SIT IN WONDER

Isis Day (age 17) — Bandon High School — Bandon

Day by day I sit in wonder about

the world but sadly the same

thoughts run through my mind

I live in a cold place by the

sea line.

I go to school but part of me still

Feels like a tool or a fool

HOW IT IS TO LIVE IN OREGON

Mark Amanya (age 13) – Harbor Lights Middle School - Bandon

First my name is Mark Amanya and I am an African boy aged 13 years for several days. I have been in America for four months in the state of Oregon. As for me, Oregon is peaceful and beautiful and people are friendly. And Oregon is not so crowded. It has a lot of different geography and environment, like mountains and deserts, different weather.

People in Oregon have a good sense of care. In Oregon there is no sales tax.

In Oregon weather changes often.

Oregon people help you to pump your own gas.

Oregon has a lot of parks.

Oregon has less traffic jams.

People in Oregon are good at living off the land. There is a wider range of hunting and fishing.

Oregon has a lot of outdoor sports.

The ocean is near in Oregon.

Oregon has the best French fries.

Oregon has nice towns at the coast.

A lot of people in Oregon know how to make crafts.

A lot of people in Oregon know how to make fermented foods like kombucha, kefir and kim-chi.

Oregon has a good seed saving community.

Oregon has the best rest stops.

Oregon has the best maintained roads.

It is cheaper to live in Oregon than other neighboring states.

BEACH

Michelle Coffee (age 18) – Pacific High School – Port Orford

The beach has sand that feels good on your feet when it is dry. The beach has ocean water waving upon it. Those waves should not have your back turned toward them.

The beach has agates, drift wood, muscles, sea anemones and sea stars if you get to see any. The sea stars are really fun to touch. I love going to the beach because the beach has a beautiful way of sharing its beauty even when the sun goes down and gives you the beautiful orange/red sunset which is gorgeous. The waves can be more than 50 ft tall with 35 to 65 mile winds.

To me the beach is one of the nicest places to go for a walk. I also like going into the woods. The water is fun for getting your feet wet and scuba diving, surfing, and boogie boarding.

ABOUT GARY CARTER

Gary Carter was born in San Diego, California in 1938 and graduated from Sweetwater High School (National City, CA) in June of 1956. After serving three years in the United States Marine Corps he attended Grossmont Community College and San Diego State as a botany major. His poems have appeared in the Las Vegas Sun and the Port Orford News as well as many poetry journals and magazines, and he is the author of three novels and two books of poetry. Gary lives in Port Orford, Oregon, where he operates a small plant nursery in the summer and does his writing in the winter. He is the father of four, the grandfather of 12 and the great grandfather of 14.

ABOUT THE PRESS

UNSOLICITED PRESS was founded in 2012 by three writers/editors who couldn't stand the way writers were treated by large publishers. The team works hard to produce outstanding works of fiction, poetry, and creative nonfiction with zero care about turning a profit. Learn more at www.unsolicitedpress.com.

CPSIA information can be obtained
at www.ICGtesting.com
Printed in the USA
LVHW01s0222090918
589567LV00013B/831/P